Mother Land

Mother Land

Poems

Linda Parsons Marion

Iris Press
Oak Ridge, Tennessee

Copyright © 2008 by Linda Parsons Marion

All rights reserved. No portion of this book may be reproduced in any form or by any means, including electronic storage and retrieval systems, without explicit, prior written permission of the publisher, except for brief passages excerpted for review and critical purposes.

The quotes on the section pages of this book
are by Theodore Roethke, *Words for the Wind* (1957).

Cover Illustration Copyright © 2008 by Rachel B. Travis

Iris Press is an imprint of the Iris Publishing Group, Inc.
www.irisbooks.com

Design by Robert B. Cumming, Jr.

Library of Congress Cataloging-in-Publication Data

Marion, Linda Parsons, 1953-
  Mother Land : poems / Linda Parsons Marion.
     p. cm.
  ISBN 978-1-60454-203-5 (pbk. : alk. paper)
  1. Mothers and daughters—Poetry. I. Title.
PS3613.A745M68 2008
811'.6—dc22
                                             2008003260

Acknowledgments

Grateful acknowledgment is made to the following publications in which these poems first appeared.

Appalachian Journal: "Madame Alexander"
Asheville Poetry Review: "Above the Esso"
CALYX: "Wedding Poem"
Connecticut Review: "For My Brother, Who Did Not See"
Grist: "Animal," "Mother Land," "Shirt Tail"
Louisiana Literature: "Sharp," "Hellebore, Divided"
Nimrod International Journal: "Ground Time"
Phoebe: "Letter to My Mother"
The Pinch: "Reminder"
Poem: "My Inner Earth," "Old Seeds," "The Great Oak"
The Potomac Review: "Rosemary, for Remembrance"
So to Speak: "New Words"
This I Believe website (National Public Radio): "Credo" (as part of an essay)

Many held the lamp as I entered this book's shadowy places and emerged into sun. I am deeply grateful for the open-armed support and guidance of admired poets and friends Katherine Smith, Judy Loest, Heather Ross Miller, Marilyn Kallet, Ted Kooser, Claudia Emerson, Steve Holt, and Jesse Graves. Equally my artist daughters, Elayne Pope and Rachel B. Travis, who counter my too-serious steps, delight me in their flowering. And those who have listened long, my warm circle: Paula Kyser, Linda Weaver, Mary Touchton. Thanks to my mother, who unknowingly set me digging for the why and the how; my Grandmother Mac, whose faithful ground I walk on; my father, who took me in; my stepmother, who opened the door. Always, Jeff Daniel Marion, my dearest and wisest companion, my eagle-eyed reader, who shows me daily what it takes to reach the summit.

For the women who steadied my ground

Contents

Credo xiii

I

My Inner Earth 3
Unearthed 4
Eleven 5
The Force that Drives: Dream 6
Running from Blood 8
Mother Wars 10
Aqua 11
Sharp 12
Letter to My Mother 13
Young Once 14
Hellebore, Divided 15
Old Seeds 16
New Words 17
Madame Alexander 18
Fan Dance 20
Rosemary, for Remembrance 22

II

Repossessed 25
For My Brother, Who Did Not See 26
Above the Esso 27
Shadow Journey 28
My Stepmother Takes Me to the Fair 29
Rescue 30
Fabled Ground 31
Animal 32

Pickle Grass   33
Ambrosia   34
Divide and Conquer   35
Mother Land   36
Sweet Rot   37
Leavings   38
Diagnosis   40
Reminder   41

III

Treatment   45
Swaddling   46
Railing   47
All that Glitters   48
My Mother's Purple Phase   49
Album   50
Where Breasts Come From   52
The Truth About Breasts   53
Coming to That   54
Standing, Standing   55
On the Line   56
Savior   57
Church of the Risen Lamb's Ear   58

IV

Dinner on the Grounds   61
Bed   62
Wedding Poem   63
The Great Oak   64
Dirt Gardener   65
Music Lesson   66

The Name of the Place 67
Translation 68
Self-Addressed 69
Shirt Tail 70
Mirage 71
This Digging 72
Ground Time 73

Credo

*I believe in the bicycle of forgiveness, the potholes
barely missed and jarred over, stickiness of new-laid tar
sucking my speed to a crawl. I believe in silver spokes,
unswerving wheels bouncing me along, though the way
forward is fogged in false hope. I believe in the way—
that if souls are reincarnated, I chose you for my mother,
chose the rutted road we've traveled/travailed, chose
the misfiring in your head, manic/depressive charge
that drove me through Alice's looking-glass, under quilts,
behind chairs until stormclouds lifted. I believe in gravel
slung, wedged in my Keds, for limping and bruised I can
salve others' woundedness, pick the rocks from their knees.
I believe in highways simmering ahead like heated lakes,
mirage of reconciliation near enough to imagine. I believe
in roadside angels: grandmothers, aunts, friends, a stepmother
who rescued strays from traffic, raised me without blood
boundaries. I believe in torque, the physics of angle and altitude,
in slamming the pavement to make time, knowing in my heart
of hearts forgiveness has no schedule, no map, no AAA
triptych. I believe in the small bell, the night's music hushing
my child's fears that fifty years have not extinguished. I believe
in the night, haunts heard only by the misbegotten, for later
comes the peach morning. I believe in the fickle wind renewing
my hair and ears, its shifting horse latitudes and rainbow
arch. I believe in the endpoint lowering its heavy barricade,
in your faith's Savior waiting to pick you like a field flower,
your goodness reborn. I believe I will stand at the opened earth
and grieve for the wasteland we've ridden far and wide,
light slanting on hills we never stopped to admire. I believe
grace will carry us there if we lean into the hairpin curves,
pedal hard, in life or after, beyond the blue rise.*

I

Nothing would give up life:
Even the dirt kept breathing a small breath.

My Inner Earth

My secret passageways cannot be known in hours
    or days. Lost pennies, jacks, weeping batteries—
castoffs tamped down, distill in orange clay edged
    in elephant ears not yet thrust out, listening low—
mounds of what might have beens, only ifs.
    I spill from grandmother's candy dish, mother's
upset nerves, stepmother's *red rover, red rover*
    tugging from the other side. Our coming near,
our shying away, strain this middle ground, fallow
    questions gritty on the tongue. Rooted in storied
past, my earth sprouts openhearted in the rich
    yet to be, drinks what blessings fall unawares.

Unearthed

Come midsummer I work the high ground
to remember. Succulents and lavender, all
that prospers in this mealy clay, untold lives
leached farther down the bank. I dig to weed out,
reveal what remains of my early uprooting:
Go on, live with your daddy, my mother flings
the white suitcase on the bed, jumbles shortie
pajamas with winter plaids, *Don't never come back!*
a molehill of clothes into mountains.

Rain and silt, wash me into my father's car,
my stepmother's house of sage and oak
where hydrangeas arrange their big blue bowls.
Cool bottomland, shield me from scalding sun.
Careless words, sink with marbles, rust
of argument, bittersweet rot. This refuse I unearth
to shards of day, ease back in its burying place.
Topsoil I peel open for flecks of mica deep down.

Eleven

Long the tunnel of night we drive,
my father's silence pressed like speed
to the dash and floorboard. Roadside reflectors
clip past, illuminated pages I count, lose count,
begin again. Woodland and Russell streets,
Shelby Park, yellow glider on my grandmother's
porch, pole beans we strung there for the Sunday
pot—each bright turning overtaken by dark.

My father grim at the wheel, his young wife
burned the rolls when I called: *Lift me up, take me
into your story.* More child than I at eleven,
my mother is left spinning her version. One foot
in the indecipherable past zooming by, the other
in blue-black shadow ahead, I am standing
strangely still.

With the white suitcase she flung on the bed,
I call from the chasm's dizzy rail: *mo-ther?*
falls far and flat. Her tantrums crack our common
ground, burden blood to breaking.

I am running to my idea of heaven on earth,
to my stepmother whose wings feather down
to cover me, who reads the tale of seven swans
and seven princes, the white-necked girls
released from dreamless bewitchment.

The Force that Drives: Dream

Not a mile from the filling station
on spanking-new tires, we are going
nowhere fast. Stuck in the road,
my brother and I shake our heads
at the sorry tires. *Flat as a flitter.*

   At eleven, you are old enough
to know our fathers are different men.
At your age I slammed the door
to our mother's house, shattered
my leaving like mirrors.

   Back at the station
I tell the mechanic to make it right:
Top of the line! Give me the top of the line!
something my father would say.

   Again at the wheel
we are unstuck and rolling on, proud
of my firmness and force. With the ballast
of silences weighing down the trunk,
now is the difficult night of our travels:

   where I write what my parents
said and did, to me, to each other,
without whitewashing or hugging
the center line. I drive into
the ditch of brown stormwater,
immersed to my neck in the runoff
of one childhood, peel out
on moonstruck gravel.

The pistons
are greased and hitting good now,
the blind curves mine to burn.

Running from Blood

Mother's Lament

They're driving away in her daddy's
big company Buick to live high
on the hog. Get on, then. No more
my towheaded child, dandelion curls
flying. Stomp my heart, run right to
your stepmother—she'll tire soon enough.
See if I take you back. What do you think
of such a girl, wanting another mama?
Didn't I keep house and home together
when your daddy cheated—that roving eye
sowed oats wild as a blinding field.
Divorce him, my sister said, and look
where it got us. One day you'll see
what it takes to get along. Oh, knocked
down and blue I am, my good girl gone!
In your new room with ruffled curtains,
do you dream of sweet things—
or of branches coming alive, tangling
your feet, clouding the way to sunshine?
Think of me in troubled sleep, knotted
up in sheets, finding a way to hit back.
You can't run from blood. My eye
is on every hair of your head,
little sparrow, first blood of mine.

Daughter's Reply

Set me on unshifting ground—not school
to school, house to house, nary a foothold
or rest. Come a stepmother's kind ways,
Grimm stories at night, come a father
constant and upright. Near kin I would stay,
but dread overspills the heart. Run I will,
from your mercury moods, your man
knowing my season of ripeness. Run
to settled clearing, flowered out before me.
Oh, I'm the wishingest girl, spooling
wishes for the greeny side of the fence,
for whoever offers life outshining. Sick
with grief, I look back, leave brother,
sister, cousin for this blue-eyed field,
leave grandmother's salvation, her porch
on Russell. The hurried map of my going
spread over lonely earth, bridge to stream,
moon to sun, to Andromeda's dusty crown.
Let me spin unreachable, skim the Sea
of Tranquility, step onto calm's shore.
Far from flashing temper, O mother
of mine, our bloodpath divided,
Amen, evermore.

Mother Wars

When I asked for Kraft macaroni and cheese in the blue box,
my mother knew it was war. A homemade cook, fat jeweled
her pole beans, potato fists simmering nut-brown, cloverleaf
rolls with oleo. My stepmother, bride at twenty, hip in black
ski pants, reached for Sara Lee and cans of School Days,
every modern convenience in her aqua kitchen. Weekends
in pincurls, radio rocking *Candy Man-ah*, I lapped up
whatever she set before me, pronounced it better than home.
So began my mother's attrition with Johnny Marzetti casseroles,
embittered blitz to sway my fickle affections. I craved
those distractions at my stepmother's table, feared scraping
the bottom of the bowl, seep of time through the hourglass.
Apart, still tasting my father's coffee, childish longing
too saccharin-sweet to swallow.

Aqua

It surrounded her like the sea: sofa, chairs, Formica
counter, even the melamine plates some shade of aqua,
all the rage in 1960. At twenty, she dove into life's well,
marrying my father, who hid his nine older years
behind a salesman's ease. At her round table, I swiveled
on the sherbet-colored stools, wash of blue on blue
swimming past—robin's egg, cobalt, turquoise, sky.
I brought her those days my ache for breath, startled
mouth and gills, freckled sheen dulled brown, left
my mother's house on the lee shore of shifting sands.
She bundled me in woven creel, feathered fern
and sage, our currents riding tidal surge, divergent
cloud, divining pool of far-gone cares; while I, furtive
minnow, swept along in her phosphorescent wake.

Sharp

Give me a dull knife, wary, just shy
of slicing the flesh that stops it cold.
I watched my grandmother peel this way:
Rome underbelly, thin-skinned russets
and cukes, one insistent spiral whittled
in a mound on the *Tennessean* society page,
her crosshatched thumb tough as hide.

Your mama's nerves is bad today, her frequent
weather report: partly cloudy/uncertain times
ahead. When I think of that forecast, again
I shrink under cover of oilcloth, behind
the heat-blacked stove, soft and sticky with grime.
I slide into the starry orbit of heirlooms arranged
on a plate, all of my sweetness unpicked.

If I rolled lopsided on the table, too blemished
or green for good eating; if I burned with salt
or sprouted offending eyes, I snagged the point
of my mother's tongue: *Now aren't you ashamed
of those grass stains? Stick out that lip
and cry, cry.*

Laid open and quartered, what has this mealy
heart gotten me? I admit being prone to retreat,
so practiced at receding into roosters on wallpaper.
I admit seeking solace in peacemakers, in homely
winesaps out of season. Through drawers I rummage
for the paring knife blunted by time's bone
and gristle. Well taught, I lean into the cut
with precision, my blade forged
in vinegar, cast iron, flame.

Letter to My Mother

I received the baby pictures you sent today:
my first birthday cake, arms ringed with fat
reaching for you from the lap of my grandmother.
I am pleased to see an early resemblance
to my father, since your face peers back so often
in the mirror. Years ago you burned the rest—
Kodacolors of me with a pageboy, in my cowgirl suit,
Easters with Aunt Ann in the park—gone the way
of your wedding album, my father's good looks
ripped in half, your ring at the bottom
of the Old Hickory.

You stood at the sink and lit the soft corners:
Christmas mornings up in smoke, my red rockinghorse
charred black as we nosed to the floor, rollerskates
mad-hot on the sidewalk, bride doll snuffed out
in the prime of her ever-after. Even your pincurls
and brief joy burned, baby, burned. In the dark
of a drawer, you have found a little light to send,
this child who beams at the eye of clarity,
opening a Golden Book where her story
is about to unfold.

Young Once

The relatives wrap leftover turkey and Derby Pie,
my mother hands out photographs of herself at twenty.
Surely my father, training for the Air Guard at Ft. Sumter,
snapped her on the beach towel: one leg coyly bent,
palms flat to accentuate her bust, that coveted Coppertone
glow of 1952. A flutter in her womb, I am the ticket
to duty stateside, those unlucky boys dogfighting
in bitter skies over Korea's 38th parallel. *See,*
she has written on the back, *I was young once too.*

Sleek and gilded in Carolina heat, surely her high school
sweetheart would never cheat with a Kappa Delta
nor stand before a judge and beg her to stay his wife.
Nor would she run from husband to husband, mistaking
the second for savior, burning down to her frosted toenails
for a third. No daughter of hers would cry for a different
mother, pack a suitcase to live in her father's house,
their ties bloodied and broken. No, her mind would not
roar like the downing of MiGs, nor drown the wreckage
in Percodan or Darvocet, the sting of their going
and going mirrored in the fierce surf.

This blinding day, her bones are hard and buttermilk
fed, unbuckled to feebleness and osteoporotic ruin.
Her breasts, jaunty enough to turn heads, unburdened
by cancer, not yet a lunarscape cratered by the scalpel.
From a nowhere street in east Nashville, she has traveled
to this brazen sun and broad shore. On sugary sand,
in the singular compass of my father's sea-blue eyes,
she cannot believe her luck.

Hellebore, Divided

Best to start when sun idles low
in the still-young spring, when rootball
unclenches, more agreeable to the blade.
Beside dogwood and beautyberry, shadowed
by fence and shed, their freckled songs
rouse me from winter's dull molasses.
Spread royally, one knuckles to earth
until steel and leverage chip away
her resolve, loosen outer daughters
to a cradle of gloves.

Other years I gave up before ruining shovel
and shoulders, tough-skinned old mother
rooted in meanness, clinging to a hard heart.
Just as some turn away from reunion,
open-handed mercies, until they've missed
the *Come on over here*, those baby steps
chanced across the breach: that stumbling
and pulling up with mud-scraped knees,
all pigeon-toed and quavery.

Old Seeds

Never dreaming the broad had such sparkle
left in her thighs, I hang the gourd on the fence,
backdrop to coneflower and dill. Her potbelly
fits right in, liver spots and crazed bottom
comeuppance to my rage for straight rows,
my glinting spade and blade.

Soon I'm eating my words: slat by slat
miracle births emerge, fallow to fertile,
rogue vines shadow rosemary and lily. Hourly
leaves unfurl broad faces, gourd children fatten
like thumbs pointing to their black maker—
dirt of wormy tomatoes, drought, glad soaking.

It always happens while my back is turned:
the greedy earth digests a few wrinkled seeds
spit from the old gourd, these harvested years
surrendered to gravity. Come February, I will
have circled the sun fifty summers and more.

Though I spin far, up with wing and caw,
labor tugs my body like mud-thick shoes.
Hardshelled and rattling a bit in the head,
I land near the shameless lilac. Braced
for the killing frost, I stand my ground.

New Words

Even now I can feel them, vestige of second grade,
words practiced on the dome of my palate, the first
I put to lined paper. Again I trace *house, tall, orange,*
the tongue's nib on the roof of my mouth, slender
lassos of *l*'s and *g*'s roped from the page into memory.

Looping and blazing the week's list of *o'clock*
and *appointment* on my tablet so hidden, I shone
like gold stars in my Blue Horse notebook,
held still the ill wind that blew my mother and me
from attic apartment to tiny duplex. Each year
the new girl, top speller flown to the Redbird
reading group while others faltered
back to the Bluebirds.

The quiet eye in our hurried wandering,
I set down fat-leaded roots no one else saw—
walls and floors of a gabled house, oranges
warmed by afternoon sun. Streets, classrooms,
teachers swirl, half-remembered, on the tip
of my tongue. My lessons go with me everywhere,
windblown, cursive, indelible as braille.

Madame Alexander

Her name was fancier than anything I'd heard
on the playground or in mothers' singsong calls
for supper: *Barbara Jean! Linda Lee!* A name
untouchable, royal: *Elise.* Every girl wants
a Madame Alexander, my mother drummed.
I was happy with my Ginny doll, Chatty Cathy,
Slinky. I loved Ginny's bangs and wardrobe case,
Slinky's caterpillar walk down the stairs.

Even on a bookkeeper's wages, nothing would do
but a Madame Alexander. So into our lives twirled
a pink confection—netted tutu, leotards, bendable ankles,
blond ballerina meant to spend her days unmussed
in a box on the shelf. On tiptoe with one flip, Elise
rose up as if startled by her own grace. My mother
had never owned such beauty: not me, her only child,
not this attic apartment nor threadbare past, sharing
underwear with sisters, a father falling-down drunk.

She married the first sweet boy who held her hand
in church, believing my father's Alan Ladd looks
would shine on her always. Alone in the crown
of that has-been house, we passed a short time
on Stratton Avenue, nursing such wounds of absence.
Held by nothing resembling regret or loneliness,
all I knew of poverty crawled up the drain after dark,
scurried off at daybreak. The couch my bed, broad ark
in drowning waters, kept me aloft. Her moods, neon
and lowdown, coiled about the rooms like Elise's tight-
fisted bun I unwound, braided into pigtails.

My mother still pines for the stage lights,
for whatever grail dazzles to unburden herself
of history. Sometimes I follow the banister
up three flights, amazed at the colors pouring in.
It wasn't all bad, she says. The times I fed supper
to my dolls, Hostess snowballs encrusting their rosebud
mouths. Times Elise, en pointe, lifted us briefly
to the proscenium. Times she tired of the dance,
walked flatfooted like the rest of us.

Fan Dance

I

Even in sleep, I wait for the *harummmmm*
to swing back around, drench the length
of me slow as a burning swig of Co-Cola.
The fan on full blast, sheers ripple,
my grandmother's front room on Russell.
The chenille spread pocks my cheeks,
pillow damp in the drool of drifting off.
Twisting on its foot—away, then lifting
the fine hair on my legs and arms,
the fan eases me down.

My father drives into town, leaves
animals on the bed as I nap—
white kitten, beagle puppy. I toss
in late afternoon sweat, mouth dry
from whistling my heart out:
C'mon, Peanut!
Here, Jackie!

The yellow four o'clocks yawn open.
Rattle of kitchen pots, tongues
of breezes lick me awake.

II

The couch my bed in our fitful space,
my mother's third-floor apartment
on Stratton. I lie on top of the sheets.
The fan dulls the heat closing in,
silver blades a cage my heart

presses against. The man who comes
is the kind who would sling a bag,
scratching and mewing, into the Cumberland
and brag about it. He steals air
from a wife and two children, breathes
sweet nothing into my mother's mouth.

Richard wakes me with nylons forced
over his head. I cover up to my chin,
bare shoulders smart like a woman slapped.
The stifled room pins down my breath.

III

The big kitchen fan in the house on Russell
booms good air over my aunts' gossip,
the laying out of plates, ice cracking
in just-boiled tea. My mouth on its mouth
oscillates Holly to Woodland, slung past
the firehall, the Lockeland Baptist sanctuary:
oooheeeaaahhh.

All-knowing eye, this wheel pivots
my grandmother's house, powders noses
and bedspreads with the flour of high summer.
In cool dark, I rise and paddle toward
her hymns of mercy like the wideness
of the sea.

Rosemary, for Remembrance

Said in garden lore to clear the head
and make the heart merry, try to breeze by
without stirring the pot of old suppers,
or lotion on a cherry bureau, or an airy porch
painted robin's egg blue—sachets mislaid
in the drawer of your mind. This fragrance
catches my breath, lingers like smoke on sleeves
and pants. My fingers feather down the soft-needled
stem. Prickly oils stick thumb to forefinger, shine
places I have shunted from light—the sorrowful
palm, the afraid place on the pale inner wrist.
Behind each ear I dab some like *Evening in Paris*,
pinch a sprig for minted lamb and red potatoes.

No rosemary in my grandmother's backyard
or kitchen. She cooked country, lard
and bitter greens, calves' brains scrambled
for breakfast, sugar mixed in the rice. At tables
set with gravy boat and tea-stained linen,
this bears remembrance: her steam under my ribs
carried me through the pinewoods of childhood.
I awakened to the gloss of morning, finding
I had wintered the worst. Across flagstones
I bristle like a mane, fierce in the memory
of her flowered dresses and reticence in all things
but pan-fried chicken and the sweet victory
of Jesus rising into clouds. Brush past me,
yesterdays, brush past.

II

In the hour of ripeness, the tree is barren.
The she-bear mopes under the hill.
Mother, mother, stir from your cave of sorrow.

Repossessed

The chaise floated on hot gravel, my mother
in short-shorts, turned to the stare of Sunday sun.
A sweaty Pabst cooled her copper thigh, then cheek,
then brow. She lounged next to my stepfather's
baby-blue DeVille, tailfins and power windows
I had never seen the likes of.

That day I jumped from the preacher's car, afire
with the Savior and life eternal. Brother Clyde
said I was a wanderer no more, but had strapped on
Jesus' sword, dipped in His precious blood. Heat
glanced off the grand and sinful Caddy, off
my mother's oiled legs. In the gospel light
she covered what she could of her shame.

That handsome man dragged her down, she always
claimed, down the unrighteous path. Their glory
road outshone even memory's shattered remains:
a man revving his passions, one day the Cadillac
burning rubber; the next, repossessed by the bank.

Did I see you get saved? she asks now. No,
but you were there when my head went back,
immersed in the Father, when temptation sucked us
both under—mine few and uncomplicated,
yours seared beyond blame or repentance—
when my robe rippled to the surface,
nigh as the wayward lamb to deliverance.

For My Brother, Who Did Not See

Sometimes they begin, awkward as freshmen set to reels
in gym class on a rainy day. They are my still-life now,
that day, that hour, my mother at the mirror as he shaves.

Whatever she hisses in my stepfather's ear unhinges them
to the hall, naked and quickened, bodies wired as if coupled.
It is Sunday morning or afternoon—they have returned

from crappie fishing, beer firing up their veins. A sort of
dance without bow or manners whose tempo I can slow
or spin free. Always I am dodging flow and jab, his left

hook slamming her head into plaster wall. Always the hall
a thousand miles long, my feet mired in sand or syrup,
down to you in your crib. The minutes I stand between you

and rage boiling over, now years, now dreams where I lift
you into treetops, catch the bus to Knoxville, end the tarantella's
mad playing. Let us not live crippled by memory or sight,

but in snatches of harmony hard fought: your hands on frets
birthing song, on canvas wielding light; this clear-eyed stare
in time, on the page, my rescue from the fray.

Above the Esso

Up here, I'm hidden from the customers he wants
to cultivate—Bonnevilles, Lincolns roll in to be lubed,
chamoised, topped off with premium. The stepchild
no one mentions, my grasshopper legs fold in the lap
of the Osage-orange that lords over the station. I aim
the green misshapen fruit at our apartment above
the garage, down on oil slicks and pneumatic drills,
where he and Ray and Gordie pick at tarred nails,
spit *Hey, Lardass* when I slip in a nickel for peanuts,
walk their hot-blooded gauntlet. *Come see us
when you lose that lardass.*

The moony Esso sign bathes my night pillow,
red-white-red egging on my mother's jagged
pleasures. The tree's forearms muscle me away
from her cheek raised blue as plums, the grocery list
and a ten shushed into my palm. Away to my father,
sending watermelon kisses on the phone, his tenderhearted
wife who stops for strays on the side of the road.

Though kin in scar and callous, I cannot camouflage
my smallness, braid my hair into cambium and bleed
yellow-gold. Perched above what is darkly rooted,
I drop down to rotting hedgeapples and supper call,
to all my mother knows of earth's spreading shadow.

Shadow Journey

There again, it's following the car, in our tailwind
steady as a zeppelin moored to the Country Squire
wagon no matter how fast my father snaps the curves
on the Plateau. The cloud's gray and bilious and high—
our standing joke as we snake through the Cumberlands.
My stepmother douses the scent of rain:
Maybe this time will be different.

The cloud follows us from Knoxville to Nashville
on holiday and summer visits to grandparents, to the mother
I left at eleven. Each trip, as the mountains crease
purple behind us, as we brake down Tennessee's middle
basin, ears popping in descent—it appears at my left
shoulder, foretelling my mother's black weather.

Along the Nashville skyline, the L&C Tower
flashes neon blue for clear, red for snow or storm,
ripples downward for falling temperatures. Time
and again, we drive straight into the vortex,
my gathering dread streaked salmon then indigo,
whipped like pale horsetails.

What tethered us in such turbulence, our blood
straining its ropes? What fault of mine, but to seek
refuge from the scarred heavens? No sheltering
eye in this thunderous world, inexplicable torrent
let loose on every yarrow field, every bud trembling.

My Stepmother Takes Me to the Fair

Give me again your upturned wrists that night
at the Tennessee Valley fair. Our green car wheeled
over knotted crowds and lakes, the Midway

a sequined collar, carnies' shout: *guess your weight,
your weight for a quarter.* Swoop and twitter of bullbats,
our world topsy, the Scrambler twirled like sugary scarves

in the cotton candy machine. Now our heads thrown
back, wrist to wrist under the canopy, grinding
the last of September into sawdust. We could live

in the straw with the prize lambs, crawl down
the calliope pipes, travel to Chicago with the Bearded
Lady. I could leave my brother alone in the crib,

my mother's house of mirrors I stumble through.
Foaming out of the hallway, she and my stepfather
naked, rank with beer, her head slammed in the wall

like a ball at the stacked bottles rigged to never
collapse, never win a rhinestone hat or bowl of goldfish.
Turn the whites of your wrists to me again, spin off

higher than anyone can see, drunk in the seat
of big-shouldered trees, burst of chrysanthemums
pounding our hair and surrendered faces.

Rescue

For the stray in the parking lot, she leaves
the third meal this week, but the hound keeps
shying away. My stepmother cannot sleep, worried
over rainy nights, first frost, now late October.

She talks hard to God, saying if You mean this
no-name female to know anything of love, then bring
her to my open car door, bring her all the way in.

Her father denied nursing school, would not bind
her to suffering, then my father bound her only
to him. No matter, the wounded followed her trail
of moonlit crumbs—screech owl in his cage, lamb

fed biscuits in the garage, whelping box she cobbled
for the nine puppies. And I, no less than those feral
orphans, limped to her hearth. In lines at the hot church

for cubes of Sabin vaccine, freeing green Easter ducks
my stepfather threatened to smash, unwrapping the gold
foil of stories at bed—she laid hands on my wildness,
saved the hunted girl from woodsman, forest, gasp

of the bottomless dark. Tales that carry me still
by the ruff of my neck, among the broken-winged
and lame who sniff her out, homing right to her touch.

Fabled Ground

So what if it takes all week to scalp
this land of its battlements: English ivy,
Spanish bayonet, bindweed strung mean
as wire, rocky spine to be cracked
with steel clang, trapdoor to childhood's
wardrobe. My feet planted in retelling,
by night the story lets down its hair
under neighbor's fence, aster bed
and hibiscus, nearly to Red China.

Once I believed, if I dug far enough,
I would fall through that fabled ground,
orphaned under angry red skies. No mother
to please with silence, no father to free
from his granite tower, my captive heart
pounding on and on at the gates.

Here only hellebores at the end
of my yank and heave, lady's mantle,
spirea plumped like enchanted apples,
the same old sorry tales.

Animal

In the big rancher, they won't see me
slip down the bank: Oliver and Betty Sue,
Buford and Evelyn, Richard and my mother—
and I, another man's child. The men switch
from sweet tea to Falstaff; the women
wear beehives and ankle bracelets, smash
cigarettes in their plates of cold eggs.

Face down in the long summer,
in the mesh hammock near a pond
that sucks the neck of land, I befriend
spongy clover, skim the clouded bottom.
More terrapin than girl, no human teeth
or ears, cool mud my true home,
guarded rushes.

My mother dyes her hair platinum,
then jet, to be Richard's showy conch,
his blackest obsidian shore. Their bodies
passing in the hallway spark and blind
like noon on water.

Inside my bony shell, dead quiet, only
the current of my hand ruffles grass
for the odd four leaves, night's scratch
and wail still pent up and burning.

Pickle Grass

Doubtless I was a studied child, mindful
of my mother's barometric weathers. I rarely
smiled, so she said, shoving joy like peas
into my lower lip. Summer, ill at ease
with my stepfather's people—brassy, blowing smoke
rings into the drapes—I strayed to the hammock
by the pond. Everywhere I fished for four-leafed
clovers, finding mostly what we called pickle grass.
Airy as shamrocks, likely birdsfoot trefoil,
the erect little pods we plucked and crunched,
tart and puckery as dills. Maybe those seeds sulled
me up, soured me good, recalcitrant as a shower
in dog days, belly scraping the unlucky ground,
wariness my shadow even in high sun.

Ambrosia

Make way for her moment in the sun: tropical volcano
spewing pineapples, pecans, marshmallows tiny as air kisses,
cemented in whipped cream and rare shredded coconut.
My mother carried her signature Heavenly Hash to holiday
doings and Sunday credenzas, sacrificial Tupperware
in fingers ringed with smoky topaz. Make way for the crowning
touch, candle of maraschino, for goppy mouthfuls puffing
out my cheeks. Such goodness I found nowhere else,
not at bed or bath, none for the bashful child of a man
cast aside in an unrepentant past. None for the daughter
with the tear in her heart the sweet slides through, leaving
ever more hunger, nectar hoarded for the bronze gods
her mother received like applause for the glorious
bouffant, pooh-poohing it as nothing.

Divide and Conquer

Dividing spent daylilies into palettes of twos and threes
    for summer's canvas, bowing out of the dirt
a hybrid nametag, clearly a yellow, *Afraid.* I stop in mid-dig,
    not remembering it among the doubles and spiders
from a local nursery that in June makes you feel
    you've stumbled into Giverny: dazzle of Mary Todd,
Happy Returns, Prairie Sunburst, Hyperion. Burying
    that bold-black name goes against the grain of facing it
square and hard. *Afraid,* my word for childhood, mother
    and stepfather bedding in a charged field, rocking
the innocent land. Let a man get a craw of beer, start slinging
    meanness, raw as Robert Mitchum in *Cape Fear,*
and I'm back above the Esso station, time I lived there
    with my mother, pooled in crude men and oil, cars sidling up
for a bellyful day and night. Flat in my hand, razor teeth
    whittled to bone, word planted in the far faraway.
I quarter the possible and the not, heeling in yellow-rooted
    Afraid, tamping down such imperfect soil.

Mother Land

Hereabouts we call it *dogwood winter,* late visitation
of hoarfrost singeing April's prime quick as flame
to tinder. Heartsick at the window, under quilts and wool,
I am slow returning to my garden worksong.

Today, your birthday, I put off calling, this wilted expanse
between us: ground sodden and silvered, first blood
of maple and myrtle drained into ruin. Icy misunderstandings
heave through topsoil, old as our earthly time.

By a girl's quarter moon, I sowed my hopes, my birthright
wormy, tenuous. The walls you stacked year by year
chapped and bruised our hands, drove us to the outer
bounds of what might have been for daughter and mother.

Ham and butterbeans, you tell me, for your birthday lunch
in the high-rise cafeteria, enough for dinner tonight. Candle
in your lemon cupcake, a quavery wish. You did not bingo
today, but last week won $5 with a coverall. Luck is all it is.

Arborists say the trees will tap auxiliary stores wintered
over centuries of begatting, unflag new emeralds
and russets as if never bitten. Looking out, the burnt iris
chills me, the cracked land burdens, separates us still.

Sweet Rot

How universal is rot, how inclusive. Its aroma is a rich mix of that which was and that which is not yet.
—Gunilla Norris, *A Mystic Garden*

Hard season behind me—rosy fists sacrificed to Easter
    frost, undying August, no halo ringing the milk-dry moon—
my worry-beads of weather strung here to yonder. I imagined
    the swagger of iris, lesser pinks starring the border, each
risen in turn. I should've foreseen the knockout punch,
    should've felt the crumbling floor's eventuality. Scorched
by drought or ice, the living cook down to parsnip ground,
    its simmer and salt, its gristle, dark thigh. My battered spoon
stirs earnest hope of another brightening March, the sump
    of old sorrows unrecognizable as leafmeal. Sweet rot softens
the battlements, melts daughter into mother into common soil.
    Whatever quarrel bound us now sinks fast, tangled in flaw
and regret, this roux of withering stems, spent flowerheads,
    fiery gumbo we raise to our lips with caution.

Leavings

What's left for a woman who barely notices reruns
of *Matlock* and *Little House*, who leaves the set on day
and night, never to part with its unblinking eye? Years
fogged in painkillers, now Paxil and antipsychotics,
she's mislaid my churning childhood in the aimless silt
of the Cumberland below her 11th-story window.

Gone like paper boats traveling her mind's dim channels:
the poison phone calls, accusations my stepmother stole me
like a common thief, Christmases I returned as a guest,
asking for bread, a stone given in return. Whatever bridge
or ferry that might have carried us across maddening waters
sinks in the thicket of furred cattails. My mother reaps
the aloneness she sowed spring to spring.

What's left for a daughter hoarding memory like Lean Cuisines
I found six-deep in her freezer? Navigating turbulents
bruised and toughened us; now a vaguely remembered current
washes over her days: my rushing away, my occasional return
a cold tug of regret. The difficult skiff bobs in half-shadow.
Too late our time swirls by, snags on a rough truce
of tranquilized hours.

Once she thumbed through my poems—tomatoey summers
in avocado kitchens, my grandfather's lapse into drink,
a marriage dissolving, my daughters' push and pull against me.
Where am I? she asked. Where, but in a blue hole, in riverrock
gouging my heel, prickly backs of birch leaves, white roar
drowning out my voice and direction.

Where, oh where are we headed—slipping downstream
in enormous undertows, following the bend into last sun.
I'm left to read the murkiness of depth and shallow,
pick through what broken iridescence remains.

Diagnosis

At 73, the doctor tells you what I've suspected for years:
bipolar disorder, or in the fitting older language: manic/depressive.
Now an answer to our lifelong argument, our way uphill
and thorny. You, armed against imagined wrongs; me,
your object of hatred, audacious enough to leave you
for my stepmother at eleven. Me, your trigger, the cold
barrel fingered until it was oiled black with adoration,
until killing us again and again was delicious,
as close to perfection as honey.

Last night in a dream, rhythmic yellow pulsed
before me. One step would have parted the great tide
foraging clover and violet. How easy to disturb
the herd at their zealous supper, winged army whirring
like tiny shields of light. Easier to fall into numbness
as venom bit my petaled body. Then a breeze
like a hand buoyed my chest, and I flew above the ignorant
drones and workers, the insatiable queen—arms beating
just enough to carry me to the plain, still field.

Pricked awake, I'm through skimming the yard,
tense and barefoot, through running in thistle, every
moment a sting near at hand. The slightest wind
tilts me over primrose and pink night, released
to the world's bitter sweetness.

Reminder

When I prop my right foot on the chair,
I slip into late July drought, the yard nearly
tinder, my hurry to water the neediest—
begonias, impatiens. Though stung months
ago, the knot burrs deep in the ball of my foot.
Small arrows in my next imperfect step,
reminder of the natural order of bees.

At the tail end of summer's ambrosia,
what sweetness the earnest workers build
in their dark boxes. I ran, as we all run,
leaving shoes behind, into pinprick of thistle
and hive, for one sniff, one embrace,
before time fell dead to winter.

Reminder of thoughtless act, stay clenched
a month more, remind me of dahlia's redheaded
pleasures, leafmeal so soon, how momentary
and constant our dangers, how fragile
our direction, uplifted and powdered, our flight
through earth brief as a sneeze.

Reminder of all other sticks and stones,
let me hang the thin-skinned poem of childhood—
my leaving home, my running away. Let me
step into that wasted light where my mother
stands washing her hands of me. Though
it works its way to the heart's weak muscle,
barefoot and careless, I brush off the stinger.

III

I can hear, underground, that sucking and sobbing,
In my veins, in my bones I feel it—

Treatment

First the tops of my feet, twinge of a nerve
disturbed; next, the prick in my forehead,
vibrating slightly. Now I am lightheaded
with lavender and sandalwood, satisfaction
a hum all through me. Shoba and her needles,
at my pulse points, loosen the body's *chi*,
swollen confluence of denials, gnarly grudges
dammed like lakewater behind my chest wall.

Ol' Arthur's got me today, Grandmama
wrung fingers so expert with crochet hook,
rain predicted in her leg, vein-roped with pleurisy.
To purge whatever's got hold of me—bursitis,
arthritis—I have pumped eight-pound weights,
arched my back into fish and cat, practiced
the exercise of the corpse on a rubber mat
to gentle sounds of the surf and bamboo flutes.
I have supplicated myself to the nightlong
moan in my hip that will not be stretched
or iced or prayed away.

Shoba says further treatment would realign
my energies like floodtime, unlock the ache
in my gateways. What lodges between hip
and pelvis to block my meridians is foreboding
older than oceans. Slung every which way
on my mother's manic waves, the gifts
I brought—flowered scarves, embroidery,
my shiny penny face—only sharpened her tongue,
buried deep this thorn. Someday I'll bleed
it out in pinpricks on a warm, scented table.
I'll lie down unafraid with her darkness.

Swaddling

for Paula Capps Kyser

Begin at the sole and instep, you tell the aide, winding
the stretch bandage around your mother's tender foot.
This is done to reduce the build-up of lymph tissue
congregating in her little bird legs, scarlet and swollen
nearly to the knee. You are teaching the young woman
to wrap your mother's legs because you cannot be there
day and night to relieve the pressure, to lift each hot limb
in your forearm, swaddle it like an orphan.

Lifted from hard life by others, our mothers are not
so different, both hobbled now—congestive heart failure,
osteoporosis—both unschooled in the maternal. Yours taken
under neighbors' wing, left motherless by pneumonia
at three months. Tom and Little Kate spun the darling
girl in her dancing shoes between them. My mother,
frog-gigging summers on Babe and Slim's farm, spoiled
rotten on sugar biscuits, the one sweet rescue
she recalls from her father's drunken reach.

I watch you crisscross up the leg, tight enough
to press the excess fluid through the exhausted veins.
She surrenders to you as she never did before, and I envy
the way you kneel and bend into her decline, needed at last
for your science, your firm hands, repairing inch by inch
the fencerow of distance. If this was my mother, our hard
years wrapped in razor wire, I might still be circling,
unsure where to place the gauze, or how best to bind
our torn horizon, not knowing if the ground I touched
was minefield or the soft hay of manger.

Railing

Together this Christmas, my mother and I search for
some peace on earth. I wind back to 16th and Russell,
dilapidated Eastland where she was raised raggle-taggle.
Years past their dying, O for another hour with my grandparents:

Mac buying cheap amethyst rings at the Nashville Arcade,
Marie's uppers soaking in a Duz detergent glass, kiss
flat as a biscuit top. Whenever my mother's harsh winds
blew me sigoglin, here I landed and begged to stay.

Gentrification surges through the old neighborhood:
shutters taken down, columns added, soffits and clapboard
spruced up with dove gray. In the alley trash, cockeyed
on holiday wrappings—the railing from the front steps—

wrought iron chipped and gouged by my cousins' saddle
oxfords, our swinging on the black enameled spokes, freed
from the church house. How hard could it be, moving
the thing to Knoxville: blankets, rope, a borrowed pickup.

How fine it would look in my garden, staked with clematis
and sweetpea, those crystalline days again scrolling bright.
My mother will have none of it, digging in the garbage
like beggars, bringing neighbors to their windows and telephones.

She wonders what thievery I have come to, and no matter
which way we turn, we're back at railing, the cold clang
bitter in our mouths, scarred relic withstanding all time.

All that Glitters

Once I joked about your beehive and jangly bracelets,
rooms of cheap brass, a cocktail ring on every finger.
Dressed to the nines in suede heels or slingbacks, you looked
down your nose (a nose we share) at my Earth shoes, ugly
and functional. Even now, you tell Brenda at the Cameo shop
Try Honey Fusion or Sheer Diamond, my hair streaked
gray, my personal henna. You knew I would never be
your kind of woman, who could hook a man
with the arch of an eyebrow.

It took me years to see that shabby house on Russell,
no tinkers for you or your sisters, precious little coal
and meat. Under all that mascara and shimmy: your mother
hunched over the factory machine, father passed out
in mid-afternoon, grandmother's feet blacked
with sugar diabetes. Your dreams only for escape
into love, some roustabout promising a platinum
tomorrow. The distance and speed between you
and that street fishtailed on sparkling gravel
left me blinking, small in the glare.

The Crystal Cathedral's *Hour of Power* says
you are forgiven of worldly bruises, indiscretions,
will someday walk on crushed pearl and gold. A promise
of reward awaits you in the throne's abounding
grace, and not in this puny life.

Beyond the glitter, I see that all we have is disputed
ground in the here and now. We walk into whatever
light waves us through, neither stardust nor beatific
blossoms, blessed even so, along our stumbling way.

My Mother's Purple Phase

BJ Thomas lovesick on the radio, so lonesome he could cry.
My mother believed not a word—left with two babies,
a mortgage, no job, a cheater she'd take back in a flash—
she could've written her own country song about a bad girl
done good, a good girl done wrong.

Thanksgiving, she and the children ate Shoney's turkey dinners
in the car, too ashamed to face her sisters, their upstanding
husbands, her mother who always knew Richard was trouble.
No one could say why he left for a Clairol blond with a budding
girl my age, another rhinestone in his string of heartbreaks.

In every room she sang Hank's purple sky, his whippoorwill
and falling stars—purple couch and throw rugs, crushed-velvet
chairs, afghans and bedspread. Though her night was long
and crawling by, something shouted in that royal color:
scant music wrung from last year's vintage, those few drops
remained of refusing silence, vinegar on my mother's tongue.

Album

> *Blackbird singing in the dead of night*
> *Take these broken wings and learn to fly*
> *All your life*
> *You were only waiting for this moment to arise.*
> —The Beatles, *White Album*

I

Lo these many years, what did they see in the dead of night,
so cold their teeth ached? A hurried figure, flannel gown
dragging beneath her coat, loafers, a suitcase—this girl coming
into the Scot Citgo on Gallatin Road, past one. At ease
by the Pepsi machine and Pennzoil rack, shooting the breeze
till closing, the three men shifted like a herd of one mind
while I dialed the phone, pulling out their grease rags. No one
spoke under the jittery fluorescent tube. Fear crackled around us,
the icy plateglass shrinking, sweating. I waited and waited
for the car, calling a friend instead of my father, waited to fly
from the empty bed up the street, my mother sleeping off
an office Christmas party. Laughing in my heart because
she would be left with the presents, not knowing where
I'd gone nor remembering her jealous spite. We were turning
down the spread when she said it, this thing of my stepmother
and me, hot words burning through my body:
Somebody said you were laying with her.

II

My mother returned the gifts: the *White Album* I'd asked for,
the white coat she still talks about, so pretty and furry,
something Jayne Mansfield might have worn. Christmas 1968,
I was fifteen, refolding my beaten wings in a gas station

where three men shuffled their feet in discomfort
under the naked sputtering light. Somewhere in the dark
black night were hidden stars, a brilliant opening to see
through, somewhere mother and daughter mended the breach.
Together we toasted the vastness, tiny room of strangers
and stale Winstons, not knowing when morning would appear,
who would stand vigil in such dire times, nor the blows
we might endure until our moment arose.

Where Breasts Come From

My mother looked me up and down,
oddity of adolescence budding in places
she once bathed straight as a stick.
At eleven, I had left her to live with my father
and stepmother—that woman, she hissed,
that thief. Our distance rusty, unforgiving
as barbed wire, wherever we touched
we drew blood.

I left her the gown of my youth stained
with clover and sour milk, echo of *swing the statue*
on far summer lawns. The straw-haired girl
with chubby knees returned a landscape
translated to hills and slopes.

Show me, she said. *Let me see your breasts.*
She named aunts and grandmothers—
surely Barbara or Marie or June had endowed
such wonders. *Show me*, she said, and I lifted
my blouse like starved petals to the sun,
as if we two were seed and pod, her body
a shell, my nascent heart feeding within.
I showed her the breach we labored long
to bring forth, the child she let slip
through her fingers.

The Truth About Breasts

In the time's backward science, doctors had assured
her mother only radiation treatments would repair
the left breast's inversion, a pucker that age surely
would have smoothed to satin. The years were ever
a friend to my mother—when she stood at the glass
and flirted, it winked back like the men shoving to be
close in her company. All that changed since the surgery,
since the heel-clicking handful of a woman she once was.

She called me to the sunless plain of her chest,
ridden down to knobby sternum and ribcage, the ruins
reflected there with our troubled past. *Look hard*,
she said I must finally see the spoils stolen at a gallop,
what the scalpel scythed like bounty, *cancer*
seared in red heartwood.

I looked straight into the cratered mastectomy,
skin stretched glossy across bone, fine azure veins.
She showed me the violence done to us that we do
unto others, the world's snarl and grab for the fullest
blossom. At the jagged image of suffering—
its silver flaking off, tissue laid open—I paid
in flesh for the years I turned tail and ran
from our fresh and tender wound.

Coming to That

> *Many people are tender of their resentments, as of the thing nearest their hearts.*
> —Marilynne Robinson, *Gilead*

I was coming to that, my husband quotes Ole Fred when I note
the stacks of dog-eared catalogs, books and magazines unread,
our own leaning Pisas. It's human nature, coming slowly to things
undone: crabgrass in the lily bed, cobwebs crisscrossing the eaves.
I take down the hatbox moldering in the closet, rim stained with time.
My mother takes down a twin box, ancient dust flying up her nose,
dirtying her fingertips. On the topmost shelf, we stored and preened
these resentments, pressed the tender love to our cheeks, promised
never to part. Our hearts grew lean on such cold suppers. I think
less and less of the silver cord that once tethered us, the veil
transparent as millers wintering in the mink trim. I can still reach it,
teetering on a footstool, I can come around, finally see it's no use
to either of us—the striped cardboard gnawed by weevils,
the grievous tulle collapsing when I touch it.

Standing, Standing

This is my church now, these are my people, my mother attends
vespers in the high-rise basement with Margaret and Lou,
neighbor ladies she halves my apple cake for, my dill chicken
salad. Wednesdays, she veers down the beige hall, tapes
new signs for the service, places a songbook at each seat.
It's all she can do to reach, that devil osteoporosis grinding
her spine and hips to meal, breastbone accordioned to her belly.
Once charismatic was almighty, going dewy-eyed
for the dark-headed ones—Brother Ralph, Brother Outlaw—
spitting image of the wayward husband who left for a bottle blond.
The basement works fine, no daughters or son disappointed
in her failings, reminders of the many rows her bitter tongue
has sown, reaping bitter wheat. When the yellowed piano begins,
she gathers breath to join the frail song, copied from the old
Broadman, standing on the promises that cannot fail,
standing on the fullness beyond earthly travail.

On the Line

Above the tumbled river, her past grays in early mist.
She picks at it like a bluecat dredged from depths—
sweet meat of regret flakes into pieces; her underbelly
hooked on men and raw desire, flung to parch on the bank;
rainbowed daughter crossways in her throat. Life's errors
soon eddy out of reach until meeting the broad Tennessee.

Between gravelly announcements of vespers
and April birthdays on the intercom, my mother
considers another day in the *Penthouse*—as she calls
her 11th-floor apartment rising over the brown Cumberland.
No lawn to mow or petunias to save from drought,
room enough to sleep, eat Stouffer's lasagne on a TV tray.

Maybe today, extra loaves from the Sunbeam truck
for the many on her prayer list. Tonight, old-time
singing in the common room. She'll be a fisher
for those not yet on the line for Christ, for those beached
and thirsting: O you stranded on desperate shores,
fear not His marvelous waters. Be drenched
in the bright fountain, wade up
to your yearning heart's core.

Savior

What stayed her hand from razor or overdose those years
the demons stormed her brain—not children or grandchildren
or the promise of another sun. Surely it was the Savior's nod
of disapproval, His luxurious hair tossed skyward, the thought
of not entering the tent of velvet brocade and kissing His sandals,
not feeling the shepherd's crook steering her to eternity.
So this is what saved her for our flesh-and-blood battles, kept
her feet planted in guile. I should be grateful, for a ghost-mother
cannot soften or finally come around to the real story, warts and all,
cannot transform a tower of salt into the shared cup. If we are blessed
enough to shout salvation from the riverbank, from a grandmother's
avocado kitchen or a stepmother's table, we've found a little
heaven on earth. We may yet hope to be lifted up, unawares,
in this daunting life or the next.

Church of the Risen Lamb's Ear

Bright tolling as any tower bell, my call to worship
in the backfence chapel of pinebark and Lenten rose:
I am bound to study the just-opened tansy, yellow offering

for the alms basket, to set straight the catmint gone astray.
My mother asks what church, how often, as my grandmother
before her, disillusioned by the faithlessness of men. Women

immersed in the One True Word fretting I will not be swept
up with the righteous at Judgment's first light, worried more
over my eternal wanderings than the slings and arrows

of this human plain. Hours before bees stagger blind
to their sweet bye and bye, I come to matins, neither maker
nor redeemer of garden weed or hymnody. Straw hat in hand,

unworthy I stand in the windflowers, in the sun's slow declination,
to receive the many oaken mansions. I pray without ceasing
for ozone and heaviness of air, for the merciful hem of rain

to skim the closed ground. Church built on sanctified riverrock,
brown bread of its altar broken, multiplied for the hungry. There
I'll be, fired up in the rows with variegated tongues of hosta

and arum. Praise to our thrumming glossolalia—Kentucky
Wonders, Israel heirlooms, the blood-red rose—all that labor
brings forth for the least of us, the earth our last revelation.

IV

The round home of a root—
Is that the place to go?
I'm a tune dying
On harsh stone. An Eye says,
Come.

Dinner on the Grounds

Come to the loaf of my gardens, salt risen
    in Fahrenheit, rising still in the upended soil
through dog days and hunter's moon, the rim
    baked bronze, center airy with cosmos. Come
when earth is sliced right from the oven, when
    lavender's exuberant honey catches on workpants,
sweetens life for hours. The butter of Mary Todd
    daylilies sizzles along the walk, dusts chin
with remembrance, softening the crust. Come high
    and lowly, magnolia and ribwort, all to the table
set with lacecap hydrangea, the best blue plates.
    Rest in lemon balm and rosemary, evening steeped
like rosehip tea. On the homeward road carry
    the glove stained mulberry, reminder of lapsed
communion renewed. This yeasty ground kneaded
    to its two-fisted heart, come to what feeds the bent
body, the unknown reaches below, what countless
    crumbs we follow on faith alone.

Bed

So handy with the well-turned word, you ask
    Headboard or footboard? Maple or cherry?
when I say I'm building a new bed. All my waking
    thoughts on this resting place: royal purple buddleia
for pillow, oakleaf hydrangea to brace winter-hard
    dreams, mondo tufted as chenille. Carved from fescue
and plantain, mulch counterpane smothers grief,
    worry reeks of potash. Here I stretch out on the ticking
of day's end. An old rhyme comforts: four angels
    at my head—one to guide me, one to pray,
two to bear my soul away. The armillary, quilted
    in verdigris, points south to June games ringing
past nine, tag of *home again, home again,*
    down thrown off to glory of morning.

Wedding Poem

for Danny, May 23, 1998

On this day unlike any other, I wanted to trail
my words in satin and tulle, barely touching
the ground as I met you there. I would gather
them, snowy as a veil boxed under the eaves,
dust of my old days shaken off like late sleep.
I would come early, gardenias in hand, running
toward this moment—but the rain has stopped,
you've taken the mattock from the shed.
Malachite dirt washed years down the grade
to the lap of the yard, white-collared fothergilla,
determined snakeberries, tree peony's deep
patience of a rock—I would wear them like linen
on this flowering day, but you've called for rosemary
and lemon thyme, whatever adds essence
and blooms without end. You've called for
the best of our planting, sewn by the candied moon,
dropped like Hansel's crumbs on the waters
ever flowing past our door. So I bring you
my sweat and skinned knees, dew-beads
on the shoulder of morning, tender place
at the small of my back, my bending down
and my groaning up, the steam we make
on the windows steeping tea, the great goodness
of table wine, your mouth on mine telling
how we will live from now on, our feet
in the red-tipped grasses, the earth's ripe belly
green as a May bride.

The Great Oak

All sixty glorious feet of her downed by whim
of wind, my own roots rip from the bank, yawing
hole in my breast, heartwood splintered, groan
of land resounding. Years I've hauled stone
and compost, wand of my grimy hands conjuring
catkin and paperwhite, small deaths, many risings.
Knee-deep in flotsam, I wade the despair
of my gardens. Lost, our wedding magnolia,
bridalwreath, dogwoods bloodied at palm and heel,
yard hobbled to its clay beginnings.

When disaster roughs us awake, Bobcats rumble
and level the field. The house narrowly missed,
the wild story told backward and forward:
How people buzzed around the beanstalk that surely
pierced the clouds, searching the thicket for golden eggs,
enchanted harp. The chainsaw's high lonesome
like a strange species of locust, neighbors circling
back to their hives, grateful for an ordinary supper,
the marvels of electricity.

We never see it coming, the ground yanked
from our footing—though I have stood here before,
in the wreckage of childhood and marriage,
held fast to the eye as thunder tolled its doom.
In this upended country, light stuns with possibility.
Among sunken islands, I row out with spells
I once knew, leaf by broken leaf.

Dirt Gardener

With those hands, you should play the piano
    I've heard my whole life, not that I haven't tried.
My music plays elsewhere—in the muck of March,
    stirring insurrection; on the trellis, maypop and trumpeter,
all sass and whirlwind, sprout from untuned rock.
    Grit seeps to quick, drives me from sturdy brick
to columbine rooms, one sunlit house to another.
    Sure as the moons I plant by, solstice signs grafted
like clef notes to bone key. High octave of glad
    and lily a barerooted memory tucked in tuberskin,
wishful thinking come spring. *Dirt gardener,*
    who deciphers the earth without hired help or design,
thumbs split on time's gnarly backside, hands
    practiced upon these scales.

Music Lesson

Betwixt and between, restless and new in my stepmother's house—
I was the child she did not plan or bargain on, only thirteen years
younger, almost a sister, my father away on business trips.
So she signed me up for guitar lessons at Pick 'n' Grin, waited
in the car while I stumbled through the streets of Laredo
week after week. My tone mournful as the drum beat slowly
and the fife played lowly, fingertips blistered, swollen with awful
repetition. *When the callous comes, you'll strum good,* said the teacher,
bored with this sodden procession. Such a natural, my stepmother
clicked the padlock of music without lesson or study. How I longed
to transpose the alien score into lightning-quick flatpicking,
soar over frets as if raised in fields of bluegrass. How I wished
to follow the hymnal, allegro then dolce to *Amen,* as if I was hers,
my tongue wrapped in white linen as cold as the clay.

The Name of the Place

> *Come on, let me show you where it's at.*
> *Come on, let me show you where it's at.*
> *The name of the place is I like it like that.*
> —Dave Clark Five

At the low-slung altar of her Magnavox console, I bowed
to their greatness, the ministers of my stepmother's music:
Louis Prima and Keely Smith, Roy Orbison, Joey Dee
and his Starliters, Mancini and Lanza. I jumped to their jive,
their strings and hangdog vibrato, popped my hips
to the peppermint twist. I wanted to be the pulse of bass
thumping, the verve of *I like it like that.* Whatever cool place
the beat sent her, I was the metronome tocking at her heels.
Dizzy and tuneless from my mother's discordance,
I wished myself into the turntable and scratchy revolutions,
into my stepmother's rouge and pancake makeup, fingers
snapping *Sweet dream baby, how long must I dream?*
The records spun dreams of waking her blood daughter,
with sapphire eyes and cucumber skin, our separateness
drowned out, our pitch pure as belonging.

Translation

Her father's first choice, the harp was too dear
for a family on Miami Street, so they settled on the marimba.
Breaking it down into tubes, keyboards, slats, she carted it
to Knoxville's moneyed ladies clubs, Arlington Baptist,
Fulton High assemblies—an oddity in the 1950s, a mere girl
hammering those rosewood bars to beat the band. Sister,
could she swing the boogie-woogie: barefoot, curled up
on her arches, two mallets in the left hand, three in her right,
sway of Tommy Dorsey sweet and hot, "Blue Moon,"
"Valencia," Brahms' Hungarian Dances, feathering
to a tame doxology for the church crowd.

All that behind her when she married my father,
the marimba in the rec room like a backstage phantom
I banged on, unable to summon such celestial sounds.
She'd pull out the old hustle when I begged, showed me
the rock, the roll, guiding my hands to accidentals above,
the naturals below. Flatfooted, clumsy, I'd failed
at guitar lessons, failed to decode the notes' march
from page to strings, to tap my chords' buried wellspring.

High C to low C, I followed thumbnails of paper
she taped to each bar. Wooly mallets rolling like Spanish *r*'s,
I drummed her morse in "Take Time to Be Holy,"
my time more funereal than divine. Though second nature
to her, I never translated the graceful signature of staff
and tempo, half-note and coda, those blessings of talent
from which all music flows. It wasn't the song
or the player I yearned to be, but the percussive wave
thrumming mother to daughter, resonance of kin
bound to kin, through the blood's anxious bongos.

Self-Addressed

Letters I remember from my father, his handwriting professional
yet stylish. He drove in and out of Tennessee on business,
sales conventions through the Southeast territory, smooth-talking
other reps into garden tillers, riding mowers. He wrote about
the day he would eat lunch at my school, appearing like a prodigal,
the movies we would see, salisbury steak at the S&W Cafeteria.
I had forgotten the self-addressed envelopes he left in my satchel.
My stepmother reminded me of his stamp to soothe the distance,
excluded from our sealed exchange, new wife infringing on precious
little time. I saw him more clearly on ivory vellum, in the flair
of his Parker 75, more at ease transfixed in darkness—Pollyanna,
Lady, Old Yeller communicating what he could not express
to a daughter across the table. Between those measured lines,
I squinted at his name inked royal blue, his deeper self
coded in foreign calligraphy.

Shirt Tail

My copies of *Siddhartha* and *Steppenwolf* dog-eared,
I was far out, liberated and braless, lolling around
in my father's blue Van Heusens. Best were those
with the sheen of starch and steambaths, cuffs not yet
frayed, at the collar a wink of Old Spice. He never
missed them—on business in Ottawa, hunting pheasant
in Kansas, or well into his cups at the Mitchell Hotel
with Jerry and Earl, freewheeling with the bosses.

No worse than the miniskirts I rolled higher
before civics class, I wore his cottons and poplins
pressed to bare skin, curved hems brushing my thighs
like fingertips, the pause of men's eyes. I wore them
when he returned to our flowered livingroom
and sank behind the sports page, when he griped
about the dry roast. I wore them until my stepmother
said, for pity's sakes, put some pants on
when your father's in the house. Oblivious we lived,
buttoned in stiff bone and pearl, in absence
and hunger, my breast pockets loose with change.

Mirage

My father took to travel like he was born in a Fairlaine,
more at home on the road than in his livingroom,
selling lawn and garden equipment across the Southeast.
His realm princely, mysterious—Art Deco downtowns,
tempura shrimp and sloe gin, firm handshakes above
and under the table, the *Yessir, much obliged* that cinched
the deal. His honeyed style glazed the asphalt, oiled
the distance he drove far and away.

In the days before seatbelts, I'd sit on his lap and steer
the car. The highway, mad-hot with summer, shimmered
ahead. *Look out!* he'd goose my ribs. *Don't get your feet wet!*
I braced every time for the old joke, wall of water
that, when we reached it, vanished on dry pavement—
mirage I never saw coming.

My father's road spiraled out like a peach peel,
the juices his alone to savor. Curves and straightaways
led him from dusk to daylight, cupped him in the grid
of latitudes. I was left with the harder chores of living,
left to discern his silences, disappearance behind
the horizon of newspaper, his concentration
still on the yellow line, at the wheel
with places to go, people to see.

This Digging

> *I can't get down deep enough.*
> *Sunlight flaps its enormous wings and lifts off from the backyard.*
> *The wind rattles its raw throat, but I still can't go deep enough.*
> —Charles Wright, *Scar Tissue*

This digging takes me nearly to the locus, but there's never
    enough lamplight to the fertile throat, the anthracite marrow.
Should I hammer old sorrows, strata by strata, until brittle as birchbark?
    Mound grit and mud for memory's pink, wet worm? Drop
a plumbline for regretted yesterdays, bubbling up around my toes?
    This digging takes me past fossil of green glass, network of roots:
split from my mother like the grief-rent of clothes; my first marriage
    severed, ghost-wife burrowed in lifesaving reams. This digging
turns me from shadow to incremental sun freckling my neck,
    summer beds drawn to full-feathered height, the chill months
miles off. I can nearly get back to passionflower roping the arbor,
    windchimes in elbow of hackberry, gourd hung as talisman
for rain. Nearly down to grace, creeping alcove to earthen shelf,
    to the deep eye of *Peace, be still.*

Ground Time

Grainy earth of mornings with a crazed cup,
my neighbor says these leavings are tonic
for what ails the acid lovers, azalea and hydrangea,

sisters of the shade. Daily I empty them in a plastic
bin, stored in the sink's cellar with Pledge
and languid oils, bottles waiting to be lifted to light.

While water runs through pipes or the soup boils
over, while I strip green jackets from basil or lose
sight of the night's dream scattered like starlings,

coffee grounds cast spells of transcendence:
Be fodder, be slops, be redeye gravy and remoulade.

Slagheaps percolate in their hothouse while I sleep
and rise and bless the neighborhood air. I open
the lid to a little volcano, lavapools spouting,

black and rank as wet leaves pressed to the spare
bone of November. This feast I spoon-feed my late
garden, small comfort for cold coming.

On rootbound beds I sprinkle verities of May,
china held two-handed to warm through and through,
necessities of cream and turbinado sugar.

While the Earth ends one day barren, steaming
in ancient argument, it wakes beloved with child,
this ground, this slow brew of time.

Colophon

This book is typeset in Centaur. Originally designed by Bruce Rogers for the Metropolitan Museum in 1914, Centaur was released by Monotype in 1929. Modeled on letters cut by the fifteenth-century printer Nicolas Jenson, Centaur has a beauty of line and proportion that has been widely acclaimed since its release. The italic type, originally named Arrighi, was designed by Frederic Warde in 1925. He modeled his letters on those of Ludovico degli Arrighi, a Renaissance scribe whose lettering work is among the finest of the chancery cursives. Arrighi was produced by Monotype as the companion for Centaur in 1929.

LINDA PARSONS MARION is the poetry editor of *Now & Then* magazine and the author of *Home Fires*. Her poems have appeared in *The Georgia Review, Shenandoah, The Iowa Review, Prairie Schooner, Cornbread Nation 2, Negative Capability, Nimrod, Potomac Review, CALYX, Helicon Nine, Atlanta Review, Poet Lore*, among others. Her work was nominated for a 2006 Pushcart Prize, and she has received two literary fellowships from the Tennessee Arts Commission, among other awards. Essays and poems have also appeared in *The Movable Nest* (HELICON NINE EDITIONS, 2007), *Listen Here: Women Writing in Appalachia* (UNIVERSITY PRESS OF KENTUCKY, 2003), *Her Words: Diverse Voices in Contemporary Appalachian Women's Poetry* (UNIVERSITY OF TENNESSEE PRESS, 2002), and *Sleeping with One Eye Open: Women Writers and the Art of Survival* (UNIVERSITY OF GEORGIA PRESS, 1999). Marion is an editor at the University of Tennessee and lives in Knoxville with her husband, poet Jeff Daniel Marion.